IMAGES OF ENGLAND

MID-CHESHIRE
PUBS

IMAGES OF ENGLAND

MID-CHESHIRE PUBS

J. BRIAN CURZON

TEMPUS

Frontispiece: The author raises a pint in the Edwardian Bar he reconstructed at the Bass Museum in Burton on Trent. The barmaid is always hard at work, as she is a dummy.

First published 2006

Tempus Publishing Limited
The Mill, Brimscombe Port,
Stroud, Gloucestershire, GL5 2QG
www.tempus-publishing.com

© J. Brian Curzon, 2006

The right of J. Brian Curzon to be identified as the Author
of this work has been asserted in accordance with the
Copyrights, Designs and Patents Act 1988.

British Library Cataloguing in Publication Data.
A catalogue record for this book is available from the British Library.

ISBN 0 7524 3852 2

Typesetting and origination by Tempus Publishing Limited.
Printed in Great Britain.

Contents

Preface and Acknowledgements

I did not need asking twice to do a book about pubs, but in preparing this book I wanted to do something more than simply compile a collection of old photographs. Instead I wanted to present a collection of the tales and anecdotes related to the pubs of Mid-Cheshire. Over the years I have been asked to sort out many an argument about the how, what and when of an old pub – usually to try to convince someone that there was no truth in the story. Most frequently told are the supposed secret passages under Winsford – and if every one I have been told about really existed then the town would have sunk without trace long ago! I do not claim that any tale here is necessarily true, or the only one, but as far as possible things have been checked and if there is no proof of the story I have said so.

Stories and tales are the main purpose of this book and so not every pub is included. The full history of the pubs is beyond the scope of this book, but A.J. McGreggor's publications list all the landlords and the dates for all local pubs. As for the quality of the ale, that is for you to judge, but the Campaign for Real Ale's publications give their (sometimes biased!) views. You may disagree with my choice of pubs, but the simple rule has been that if the pub had a tale to tell then it got included. I have refrained from writing about things that go bump in the night – being a sceptic I think many of them have more to do with the spirits in bottles than those in the afterlife! In any case, almost any old pub worth its salt should have at least one resident ghost.

You may have other tales to tell and no doubt there are different stories; as always the aim of my writing is to stimulate discussion and debate and I would enjoy hearing your old pub tales.

Especial thanks to Mike Troy, whose amusing illustrations add another dimension and interpretation to many of the tales. Paul Hurley also copied some of the pictures from originals in the pubs and took modern photographs where archive ones were lacking and Bob Curzon helped with photographs of old Winsford. Thank you to the landlords and landladies who have let me copy photographs and pictures from their walls; to the Winsford Local History Society for the loan of photographs from their archives and Cheshire Museums for items in their collections. Many photographs were taken when I first started to write weekly items for the *Chronicle* in the early nineties and they too are now becoming archive pictures!

Enjoy exploring the pubs of the heart of Cheshire but remember the advice above the door at the George and Dragon in Great Budworth:

As St George in arm'd array did the fiery dragon slay,
So might thou with might no less, slay that dragon drunkenness.

Introduction

A Short History of the Local Locals

It is uncertain when people first started to gather together for drinking and socialising in Mid-Cheshire. Archaeologists believe the first ale was brewed in Egypt. The god Bes, who helped in childbirth, was depicted in the form of a pot with a face on it. By coincidence, some Roman pots made in Northwich also had faces on them. The first evidence of ale brewing in Britain is from the early Bronze Age, known as the Beaker Period because of the large pots suitable for drinking ale that were made then.

It is likely that there were official inns called *mansios* in the Roman settlements at Middlewich and Northwich but no trace has been found so far. What is clear is that the inhabitants enjoyed a tipple - as numerous glass and samian ware cups have been found along with flagons. These round-bellied containers for ale and wine were even made in the kilns in the two settlements and large amphorae used to bring wine and olive oil from the Continent have also been found.

The first records of ale come from the Abbey of Vale Royal, and as early as the thirteenth century there was a brew house there. This made ale, which was the main drink of the monks. The rules laid down that they each had a gallon of weak ale during a normal day, but a gallon of strong ale each on special days. Work carried out for them was even paid for with 'a flagon of good convent wine'. Travellers could call in for a 'dole' of bread and ale and so many did that the Abbot frequently complained to the King that it was costing him too much!

Inns must have existed (though we have no exact details) but any farm or house of any size had a buttery where the ale butts were kept cool and most brewed their own ale. It was, after all, the only thing most people could drink. Grapes for wine would not grow here, milk probably contained germs and was wanted for cheese and well water was always suspect in an age when wells and cess pits were often close together.

The earliest records of landlords survive from the seventeenth century, but it is often difficult to link them to a specific inn. As Cromwell closed all the inns, along with theatres, it is difficult to prove continuity. In those days public drinking was usually accompanied by dining out and from the sixteenth century beer flavoured with hops took over from ale. In the eighteenth century came the age of the stagecoaches. They 'posted' from coaching inn to coaching inn and a journey from London to Cheshire would take over a week. At each inn the horses were replaced with those which had pulled the previous coach and which had had time to rest and feed. People too were catered for, with private rooms for the wealthy and communal ones for the lower classes. Several examples survive with their large stables. Throughout the nineteenth century, when pubs served railway stations, they had coaches and horses to be hired to take people on their journey from the station to their homes. Many farms doubled as places where a traveller on foot or local people could call to buy food and drink while taking a rest on their travels. Even Wesley, that founder of the teetotal Methodist church, stopped at local pubs on his missionary journeys through the country.

As the Weaver Navigation developed from the 1720s pubs also gathered around the shipyards and wharves. As with any port, even inland, there were nice and not so nice girls who loved a sailor. The riverside pubs became a 'red light district' where respectable women would not venture at night. Equally, along the canal, lockside pubs were designed as part of James Brindley's plan. They allowed stopping facilities for food, drink, to get fresh water, etc. The bargee would often have a pint inside while his wife and children, who all lived on the boat, negotiated their way through the lock. There were also stables for the boat horses to stay overnight in cold weather and eventually wash-house facilities as well. As at many times in history horses were looked after better than working people and were more costly to replace, so stables were essential for most pubs other than street corner locals.

Before education became compulsory in the 1870s many people could not read and a picture sign was used to identify pubs. This has caused some amusing changes of name as people would call the pub by what they saw, even if it was supposed to be someone's coat of arms.

The picture becomes clearer in the nineteenth century. During the wars with Napoleon the favourite tipple, at least in London, was gin; Hogarth's Gin Lane etchings record the situation. The Government felt people were too drunk on gin to prepare the supplies for the army and taxed spirits in the hope people would turn to tea and coffee, or at least beer as a substitute. Worse was to come when the war ended and men were dismissed without pensions or a chance of work. Laws restricted the access to public reading matter and forming a union could lead to deportation. The Duke of Wellington's Government responded by introducing the Beer Houses Act and taxing spirits so heavily that the working man switched to drinking beer. Many of today's pubs had their origins with this Act. However, many others were little more than a room in a cottage with a barrel of beer and a few sticks of furniture, catering for local people who welcomed the company and warmth of the fire in an age of overcrowded houses.

Of a slightly better class were the commercial hotels in which a commercial traveller might book a room to sleep in and a parlour in which to trade. They were the company reps and salesmen of the day and not the door to door salesmen who now use that title. These hotels also had function rooms for public meetings and formal gatherings as well as wedding receptions and other such functions. Many also had 'club rooms' where the friendly societies met. They were weekly gatherings of approved men for social purposes, but they also contributed to a fund to help each other in cases of illness or to provide funeral expenses. Official bodies too, such as the Inland Revenue and local Board of Health, would use part of a pub as an office and business bargains were often made over a drink and a meal in a pub. Drinking was allowed from six o'clock in the morning until midnight!

During the last decades of the nineteenth century Northwich practically wallowed in ale, with one pub for every thirty-seven people living in the town. Many of the customers were people who visited the town to work or trade or lived just outside the town boundary. Meanwhile Winsford was split between the Market Place with eight pubs in a row and Wharton where there was a utopian pub-free settlement. In the

An unusual scene of a Northwich inn interior in 1834. It shows a meeting of the Salt Association agreeing to fix artificially high prices for the salt after the abandonment of the salt taxes. Their plans were thwarted by the opening of new works in Winsford to undercut the Northwich trade. *(Courtesy of the Salt Museum)*

streets around the church there was a school, a Co-op and other shops, but no pub at all. Country estate owners controlled drinking on their property with pubs banished to the edge of Darnhall and Whitegate, reduced to one in Great Budworth and totally banished from places like Bostock and Winnington.

In 1911 the 'People's Budget' introduced the first revenue duty of a penny a pint to pay for old age pensions – it was to go up by a penny a year from then on. Things changed with the First World War. The Government had promised that the war would be over by Christmas and many men had signed up so they would not miss the fun. The war went badly wrong and some of the blame was apportioned to the workers making supplies – the war would be won if it was not for people lounging around in the pub all day. Opening times were introduced for the first time in 1914. Pubs opened for four hours to allow a drink and a meal at midday, and for four hours at night. Women were discouraged to stay longer than to eat lunch as they should be at work in the munitions factories not luring men away from their essential jobs!

Another threat to the traditional pub came from the Victorian Temperance movement. From 1893 licensing magistrates (who often supported Temperance – in principle if not practice) could take away licences if they felt there were too many pubs together. There were some streets where almost every other house was a beer house. Sometimes the licences were transferred to new pubs which were being built on the new council housing estates, but many were lost. Temperance hotels, like the one whose advert is still painted on the end of the Lion and Railway, or botanical brewers like the fondly remembered 'Pop Hornby' served the non-drinkers who still wanted to go out.

Another threat to Northwich's pubs came in the 1960s and '70s. The town was served by Greenall Whitley without exception. To cut their outlays they shut down pubs knowing that if someone wanted a drink they would have to drink the brewery's beer somewhere else. Several empty pubs and a club were destroyed by fire at the same time. It was the Campaign For Real Ale (CAMRA) which changed the situation, forcing the company to swap some of its Northwich pubs with Wilsons' Brewery by threatening to take the company to the Monopolies Commission.

Until the 1970s four pubs in Northwich had market licences on Friday and Saturday and young people flocked there every week to arrange what they would do in the evenings. It was technically a misuse of the rule, as the extra period of drinking was for market users, but it was very enjoyable for those concerned. The town's police inspector was determined to stop the extension. After numerous raids to try to catch underage drinkers, he arrested a couple of drunks on the pavement outside and the extension was stopped. From then on at 3.00 p.m. the drinkers went to the football or other clubs who were licensed until 5.00 and got two extra hours!

The law allowed optional all-day drinking from 1988 and, as with most towns, the town centre pubs now offer live entertainment for young people most weekends. As this book goes to press the law is changing again to allow late-night (or even all-night) drinking and the banning of smoking in pubs, and a new chapter in the story of drinking is about to start.

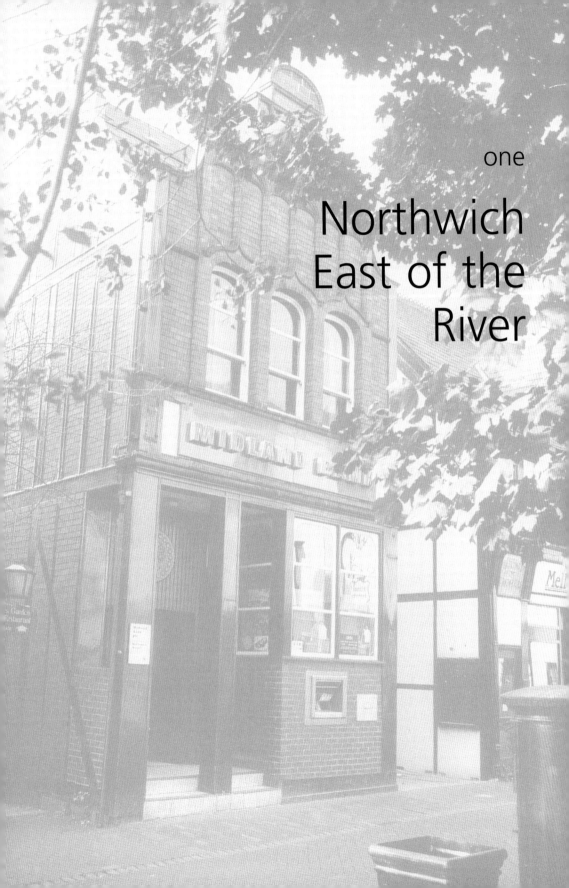

one

Northwich
East of the
River

The Bowling Green is one of the oldest buildings to survive in Northwich, and probably originated as a farm. It is actually in the township of Leftwich. The date 1650 on the cross wing is misleading as that bit was actually built to extend the pub in 1938. The date is copied from the original date over the front door. Pubs were actually outlawed by Cromwell in 1650!

When the building was extended after a fire burnt the thatched roof, timber-framed walls were discovered along with the huge open kitchen fireplace. An interesting feature in the pub, which is next to the Salt Museum, is the cupboard in the chimney used to keep salt and spices dry.

R·ROBERTS·VOLUNTEER·INN·JAN·1st·1892·No·124

Above: The Volunteer takes its name from the volunteer regiments which were formed after fears of invasion by Napoleon III of France. in the 1850s. Local regiments were formed to keep a ready supply of trained soldiers as a sort of Victorian 'Home Guard', even after the threat of invasion had passed.

Right: Most members of the volunteer regiments returned victorious from the Boer War, and were among the first to sign up and die in the First World War. After the war the local regiments were wound up, to be revived as the Home Guard during the Second World War. The Volunteer Drill Field, behind the pub, survived as the Northwich Victoria Football Club until the twenty-first century.

FIRST TEAM MATCHES.

Date.	Club.	Ground.	Goals. Won.	Lost.
1884				
Sep. 13	Preston North End ..	Preston	1	4
,, 20	Birm'ham St. George's	Birmingham..	1	4
,, 27	Crewe Alexandra......	Crewe.......	3	2
Oct. 4	Stoke	Northwich ..		
,, 11	Aston Villa	Birmingham..		
,, 18	Oswestry	Northwich ..		
,, 25	Ches. v. Liverpl. & Dt.	Liverpool		
,, 25	Chester College	Northwich ..		
Nov. 1	Witton, (Blackburn)..	Northwich ..		
,, 8	Leek (Eng. Cup. Tie).	Leek		
,, 15	Stoke	Stoke.......		
,, 22	Crewe Alexandra......	Northwich ..		
,, 29	Ches. v. Staffordshire	Macclesfield ..		
Dec. 6	Eng. Cup, 2nd Round..			
,, 13	Ches. Cup, 1st Round..			
,, 20	Leek White Star	Northwich ..		
,, 26	Wednesbury Strollers.	Northwich ..		
,, 27	Burslem Port Vale....	Burslem		
,, 29	Aston Villa	Northwich ..		
1885				
Jan'y. 3	Eng. Cup, 3rd Round.			
,, 10	Birm'ham St. George's	Northwich ..		
,, 17	Witton, (Blackburn)..	Blackburn ..		
,, 24	Ches. Cup, 2nd Round.			
,, 24	Eng. Cup, 4th Round..			
,, 31	Burslem Port Vale....	Northwich ..		
Feb'y. 7	Halliwell	Halliwell ..		
,, 14	Ches. v. Denbighshire	Northwich ..		
,, 21	Ches. Cup, 3rd Round.			
,, 21	Eng. Cup, 5th Round..			
,, 28	Oswestry	Oswestry		
Mar. 7	Ches. v. Staffordshire	Stoke.......		
,, 7	Earlestown	Northwich ..		
,, 14	Ches. Cup, 4th Round.			
,, 21	Stoke	Northwich ..		
,, 28	Ches. Cup, Final Tie.			
,, 28	Eng. Cup, Final Tie ..			
April 4				
,, 11	Chester College	Chester		

Season 1884-85.

NORTHWICH VICTORIA FOOTBALL CLUB.

President:

ROBERT VERDIN, Esq., J.P.

Vice-Presidents:

G. F. Wilbraham, Esq., J.P.	Lea Jones, Esq.
J. T. Brunner, Esq.	L. Mond, Esq.
L. B. Wells, Esq.	H. Brutt, Esq.
T. Ward, Esq.	H. H. Cook, Esq.
W. C. Cheshire, Esq.	T. Moreton, Esq.
J. Verdin, Esq.	G. Jarmay, Esq.

Captain: W. H. HUGHES. **Vice-Captain:** G. PLANT.

Committee:

Mr. J. Sanders.	Mr. J. Lowery.	Mr. P. Watson.
Mr. T. Cumley.	Mr. W. J. Yarwood.	Mr. J. O. Gleave.
Mr. F. R. Hobson.	Mr. J. Pritchard.	Mr. J. P. Hughes.
Mr. D. Molyneux.	Mr. W. Drinkwater.	Mr. A. Stelfox.
Mr. E. Fryer.	Mr. W. Bradley.	Mr. B. Dobell.

Hon. Treasurer: MR. C. J. HUGHES.

Sec.: G. A. HUGHES, **Asst. Sec.:** W. BARNES.

47, Witton Street. *22, Witton Street.*

Member _Mr. J. Wors_

Card to be shown at Gate, or admission will be charged.

W. HOBSON AND SON, PRINTERS, NORTHWICH.

SECOND TEAM MATCH

Date.	Club.	Ground.	Won
1884			
Sep. 13	*Earlestown 1st......	Earlestown ..	6
,, 20			
,, 27	Warrington 1st	Warrington ..	12
Oct. 4			
,, 11	Macclesfield 2nd......	Northwich ..	
,, 18			
,, 25			
Nov. 1	*Nantwich	Nantwich	
,, 8	Knutsford 1st	Northwich ..	
,, 15	Stoke 2nd	Northwich ..	
,, 22	Crewe Alexandra 2nd..	Crewe	
,, 29	*Over Wanderers 1st..	Northwich ..	
Dec. 6	*Haydock Temprce. 1st	Northwich ..	
,, 13	Davenham 2nd	Northwich ..	
,, 20	Knutsford 1st	Knutsford ..	
,, 27	*Over Wanderers 1st..	Over	
1885			
Jan'y. 3	Macclesfield 2nd......	Macclesfield ..	
,, 10			
,, 17	Knutsford 1st	Northwich ..	
,, 24			
,, 31	Davenham 2nd	Davenham ..	
Feb'y. 7	Crewe Alexandra 2nd..	Northwich ..	
,, 14	*Haydock Temprce. 1st	Haydock	
,, 21	*Nantwich	Northwich ..	
,, 28	Warrington 1st	Northwich ..	
Mar. 7			
,, 14			
,, 21	Stoke 2nd	Stoke	
,, 28			

* Victoria "A" Team.

Northwich Victoria Football Club was founded after a friendly match between two local teams played on the Drill Field. It was a founder of the Cheshire League and the Second Division of the Football Association, but left after losing every match in its first year! This was their first printed fixture list and ticket in 1884. The pub name honours the team even though the field is no longer there.

Above: The following pictures prove that much that has been written in the past about the Bridge Inn is mistaken. This photograph shows the building at some time between 1876 and 1896 as the landlord's name Bradley can be made out over the door. It was held together by metal plaques and tie bars even then.

Right: The same building is shown here, and in several other photographs of the subsidence in London Road, at the end of the nineteenth century. It was rebuilt soon afterwards as a bungalow and when the scientist Calvert wrote in his *Salt in Cheshire* that the barrels were hung above the bar it must have been the new pub he saw around 1900.

Left: This picture shows the new building, but the hanging sign identifies it as the Bridge Inn. It was taken when the decision had been made to move it to a safer location further south along London Road. It has been lifted on heavy sleeper beams prior to the move. The arts and crafts detail of the gable is typical of the late nineteenth and early twentieth century.

Below: This diagram shows the way that the pub was taken back and moved on rollers behind the Leftwich Brewery to the present site. The roller slides were supplied by Yarwood's boat yard on the opposite side of the road and were usually used for launching boats.

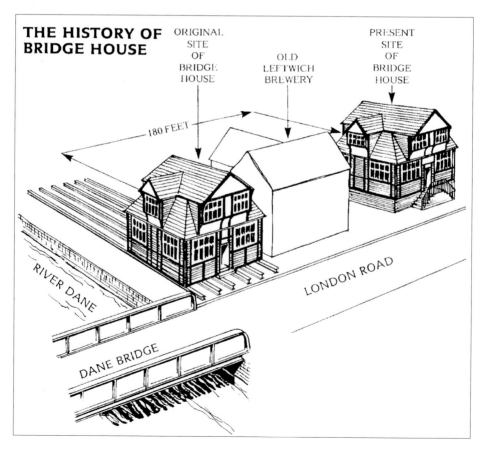

THE HISTORY OF BRIDGE HOUSE

ORIGINAL SITE OF BRIDGE HOUSE

OLD LEFTWICH BREWERY

PRESENT SITE OF BRIDGE HOUSE

180 FEET

RIVER DANE

LONDON ROAD

DANE BRIDGE

Even in its new site it was not safe and it was swamped in the flood of 1946. In 1956 it was raised onto a brick plinth to be above the level of the flood, as were all the buildings in this part of London Road. The photograph was taken in 1956 at the time it was raised. By then it had been closed as a pub due to its inadequate size.

Left: The building was used as solicitors' offices from the 1950s to the '90s and there followed a period when it was used as the Council for Voluntary Services Office. It was converted into a set of self-contained flatlets for single men by a partnership between Vale Royal Borough and the Muir Housing Group. Representatives are shown here at the reopening.

Left: There is a narrow opening leading from the Bull Ring to the River Weaver which still has the name Watling Street and is presumed to lead to the Roman ford. The Turk's Head in this Watling Street was used by boatmen waiting for orders and possibly takes its name from the decorative knot on top of barge rudders.

Opposite below: The Angel's position made it the obvious choice for civic occasions in the past. This crowd has probably assembled in 1901 to hear the official announcement of the death of Queen Victoria and the accession of Edward VII. This official announcement followed a few days after Victoria's death as a platform was assembled and people gathered to show allegiance.

The grandest hotel in town was the Angel in the Bull Ring, which was used for receptions and meetings as well as for important visitors to stay. By the twentieth century its brick walls were twisted out of shape and flooding had deteriorated the woodwork. It was closed in 1921 and replaced by the National Westminster Bank.

Until the end of the 1940s subsidences under Northwich caused fairly regular floods. This picture of the Angel in a flood shows one of the factors which caused it to become too unstable to be left standing. The misshapen windows are clear to see and the continued flooding caused the foundations to become unstable.

Lloyd's wine bar was once a butcher's shop and still has impressive plaster work showing a bull and a cow. During the 1970s it opened as Pimlott's, an upmarket dress shop, but became a wine bar in 1981 when magistrates refused a normal pub licence. In 1984 it was allowed to sell beer, but is still known to all as the wine bar.

The Eagle and Child (or 'brid and babby') is now the HSBC Bank, but the Stanley crest of an eagle and child is still to be seen in the gable. Lord Stanley was given the manor of Over by Richard III before he betrayed him at Bosworth. Another Lord Stanley camped here with the Cavaliers at the Battle of Winnington Bridge.

Legend tells how Thomas Lathom was sad because although he was one of the richest men in Lancashire he had no son to pass his titles on to. He arranged for his illegitimate son, by a serving girl called Mary Oscatel, to be tied to a tree where an eagle had nested. He took his wife that way so she could find and adopt the baby.

In the late 1930s regulars at the Crown and Anchor were intrigued by a quiet and rather reclusive guest who worked at Yarwood's boat yard on a secret project. He was Lawrence of Arabia, using his adopted name of Shaw, and was working on plans for a boat that could use radio waves to send and receive messages while at sea.

Opposite below: The baby's mother was employed as wet nurse and the baby was named Oscatel as he was so fond of her. Thomas confessed all on his deathbed and the boy was turned out. His daughter had married into the Stanley family, who used an eagle eating a child as their crest. The Stanleys lived at Winnington Hall in the nineteenth century.

The boat was used to spy on the German navy during the Second World War, but water destroyed the old pub. Despite being rebuilt in timber frame and raised during 'the big lift' in the 1920s (shown here), its cellars continually flooded and the beer barrels had to be chained down to prevent the part-full ones floating away.

In 1758 a well-dressed woman walked into the Red Lion in Northwich and demanded that the landlord find her a husband – at once. The publican suggested a barber, but when he hesitated a tailor's apprentice offered his services and went at once with the woman to Budworth where weddings took less time to arrange. As they left the church her father arrived.

Right: It transpired that the woman was an heiress with £500 a year to spend and her father had arranged for her to marry an old miser. Unfortunately the records at Budworth do not support the story. The Red Lion was rebuilt in timber frame and is now a travel agents – I wonder if they specialise in elopements?

Opposite below: The rear of the Black and White Hotel is shown in this photograph of the 1948 floods. It backed onto the Weaver and eighteenth-century travellers would continue their journey to Liverpool by boat from behind it. In 1960 it was demolished to make way for Lennon's Supermarket, which was taken down ten years later and replaced by the TSB Bank.

The Crown was rebuilt in 1924 and the crowns above the door depict the one made in 1910 for George V to be crowned Emperor of India at the Delhi Durbar. The old cellar is still in existence under the floor, but when last entered it needed a full extending ladder to get to it. The beer is now stored in a cold room at floor level at the rear.

Opposite above: The Crown actually has a street named after it, and the part to the left of this picture was use as the Northwich Guardian Office during the late nineteenth and early twentieth centuries. During the 1860s it was also used for the Petty Sessions and the County Court when the old court house was destroyed by subsidence in the 1850s.

Opposite below: Another 'criminal activity' at the Crown was the arrival of the Red Rover coach from Liverpool, taking prisoners in chains to be transported via the prison hulks at London. In the 1960s and '70s its extra hour's drinking made it the place for young people to meet on Saturday afternoon – they did not need taking in chains. If they ended up in the police cells their breakfast was actually cooked at the Crown!

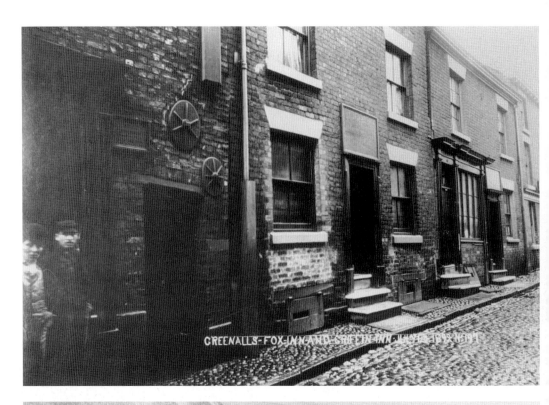

GREENALLS-FOX-INN-AND-GRIFFIN-INN-JULY-12-1899-N°19T

McCORMACK-SEVEN-STARS-DEC-11-1891-N°123

From 1768 the rental of The Queen (later The Queen's Head) was used to pay the fees of six boys from Northwich and six from Witton to attend at Sir John Deane's Grammar School, whose trustees owned it. Beyond is the Boilermakers' Arms with the trademark of Sandiford's Northwich Brewery, a cross-section of a salt mine.

Opposite above: The Fox Inn went through four name changes in the nineteenth century and closed in 1892 to be replaced two years later by a half-timbered structure. That Fox was also demolished to make way for the market car park in 1969.

Opposite below: The Seven Stars, photographed just before closure in 1911, had been in existence since 1788 when it was known as the Ship Launch. It became The Ship, then the Ship Britannia, and was the Travellers Rest before taking its last name in 1851. Along with the Fox Inn and the Griffin it was closed and the licence transferred to the Greenbank.

There are two theories about how the Bleeding Wolf got its name, but there are several examples in Cheshire and none outside the county. One suggests that it is derived from the bleeding wolf's head on the shield of Hugh Lupus (Hugh the Wolf, 1st Earl of Chester), the other that the last wolf in England was killed in Macclesfield Forest.

Oppoaite above: Chips were not rationed during the Second World War. The landlord at the Bleeding Wolf was dismayed to see his customers leaving early to buy chips. Declaring 'if they want chips they can have them here', he invested in a chip pan, fat, a bag of potatoes and a knife, which were placed by the open fire for customers to make their own.

Opposite below: The formidable lady in the door of the Bull's Head is a mystery. Above the door the name Eliza Rowbothan can be made out on the sign. The problem is that when this photograph was taken the landlady is recorded as Eliza Burgess who was landlady from 1880 to 1923. The pub stood in Applemarket where the market car park is now.

The Penrhyn Arms takes its name from Lord Penrhyn, the nineteenth-century owner of Winnington Hall and a Liverpool owner of plantations and slaves in the West Indies. It was very popular on Saturday evenings as it had more room than the bar at the Memorial Hall which stood opposite.

The Bear's Paw, shown before demolition in 1963, was one of the three-storey buildings in New Street which are believed to have had eighteenth-century loom shops on the top floor. It stood in New Street, the last eighteenth-century street to survive in the town, near to the present Seafarer chip shop. The paw is the crest of the Earl of Crewe.

The Old Ship Inn stood opposite Leicester Street on Witton Street. The weather-boarded walls made it look like a ship, but the name is older, going back to 1763. In 1933 it was demolished and the old Marks and Spencer's store was built on the site. The timber probably came from the riverside timber yard in Leicester Street.

The Local Board of Health was founded in 1874 to provide decent water supplies, sewerage and better burial facilities in order to improve the health of the people. It was absorbed into the Urban District Council ten years later but during the 1870s it made use of a room in the Talbot as its office where the rates were paid.

Opposite above: The Talbot survived until the 1960s when it was demolished along with the Methodist chapel next door, to be replaced by Victor Value's supermarket. To its rear, down the gap between it and the chapel, was a tiny burial ground with the original wooden United Methodist Free Church, known as the Tabernacle, rebuilt behind the chapel.

Opposite below: Opposite The Talbot was the George and Dragon which closed down in 1993. Until legislation prohibited men-only rooms the bar was only accessible to men and the link to the rest of the pub was through the men's 'second class urinal'. I accompanied Pam Beddard of the *Northwich Guardian* as the first ever woman served in the bar.

There is an oft-quoted misunderstanding about the White Lion. It was said to have sunk by a whole storey so that the cellar was actually the former bar and tap room. Although there were blocked windows in the brick cellar it did not resemble the first floor of this structure which is entirely of timber frame construction.

Above: The truth is that it was demolished and rebuilt at some time in the early twentieth century as careful comparison with this photograph taken just before it was demolished and the old one shows. No doubt someone saw the old photograph and did not look too closely at the structure, simply noticing the different height, so a story (or storey!) was born.

Right: The Druids' Arms was situated next to the Leicester Street mine which can be seen in the background in this picture. It is about to fall into the collapsing mine and is heavily shored up with timber. In 1909 the Salt Union paid compensation for the demolition of the building, which did not take into account the unemployment of the landlord.

The old Waterman's Arms was a small ale house, which also included a general shop and off-licence. The shop became a billiard room and, like all other Northwich pubs, it was rebuilt – this time in 1928. It took its name from landlord George Senior who had worked on the river and opened the pub in 1834.

Opposite: The dole queue after the First World War outside the Employment Exchange by the old post office. This handsome building, with its large sorting office at the back, was made redundant with automated sorting at Crewe, and is now a pub with the appropriate name of The Penny Black. Iit still has the royal coat of arms on the front for the Royal Mail.

Left: The Waterman's was renamed Witton Chimes when Wilson's Brewery took control after the campaign by CAMRA for variety in local ale. It was fondly known as Ma's after Ma Kenyon, landlady during the Second World War. When Americans met girls at the fairground behind the Plaza, Ma would welcome 'her boys' – and their food parcels.

Below: An interesting group of buildings were erected at the same time as Northwich Station in Station Road and were built in 'railway station' style with contrasting bands of coloured brick and arched windows. The chapel and shop have been demolished leaving only the Green Dragon today.

This is the only reliable photographic evidence of a pub sinking in Northwich and shows the Forester's Arms, where Queen Elizabeth House is now. Many friendly societies aimed to prove they had ancient origins, but that of the Forester's asserted to be the most ancient of all, claiming to have been founded in the Garden of Eden.

The Cock Inn was on the boundary between Witton and Northwich, although the exact location where the change takes place is now uncertain. It is officially in Witton Street, but is away from the signs for Witton Street and Station Road which are a distance apart outside Queen Elizabeth House, so it appears to be in Station Road, according to the street signs.

Opposite above: Being outside (though apparently inside!) Northwich, the Cock Inn escaped the bye law which ordered all new buildings in the town to have a timber frame. This structure dates from 1932 in a solid 'road house' style appropriate to the depression years. It became a centre of evening entertainment in the 1980s as a cabaret bar.

Opposite below: The fine roundel of a gamecock might have been saved from the entrance porch of the old pub. Since the building of Queen Elizabeth House there have been objections on the grounds of noise and when it was used as a cabaret bar in the 1980s the police took away the licence. Though it later reopened, it is currently empty with an uncertain future.

The Lion and Railway has a joint name to prevent confusion with other railway pubs. It was opened to take advantage of the travellers using the station, providing accommodation and also stables to leave or hire a horse when coming to or leaving the town. Its curved frontage looks as if it was intended to have another building adjoining it.

The room upstairs was used until 1958 as a chapel of rest by a local undertaker. It was painted in sombre dark greens and browns, but a pub with a corpse upstairs must have been ideal for a wake. You could have a dead drunkard upstairs and dead drunk people mourning for him downstairs!

The Townshend Arms took its name from the Townshends of Wincham Hall but tragedy struck as the flashes (pools over collapsed mines) extended slowly to the rear of it. A boat was always kept tied at the back so that a rapid escape was possible. Eventually it was decided to close it on 10 July 1913 when water was lapping at the back door.

During the following night the pub sank slowly below the waters of the 'flash', never to be seen again and the next day its licence expired! Because of the old name 'wych' for a salt house it was usually referred to as the Witch and Devil. It was popular with anglers and others who came to enjoy its waterside position.

A new pub was built on (hopefully) safer ground and is now the popular Salt Barge, which provides comfortable eating in large rooms. It is convenient for visitors to the Lion Salt Works. It was built on a safer site, but it backs onto the filled in flash and on the other side of the canal bridge there is the water-filled site of the Marston Mine.

two

Castle Hill
to Sandiway

Retracing our steps to the other side of the River Weaver in Northwich we come to Castle Street with Castle Hill above it. On the left of this picturesque view can be seen the Sportsman's Arms. At one time it was a large popular hotel with club facilities, stable yards and guest bedrooms.

Unfortunately lack of investment at the time when Greenall's owned all the Northwich pubs saw it become more and more neglected. It was let for a time to a number of retail tenants who did not spend anything on its upkeep and so deteriorated even more. Having stood empty for a while, a series of fires put it beyond repair.

The old Wheatsheaf was beside the Sportsman's Arms and was a substantial pub with stables for seventy horses, however the floor of the tap room collapsed and three men were left floundering amongst the floating barrels in murky water. Its name and licence was transferred to an old beer house called the Cheshire Cheese fifty feet away and the new pub was built behind that.

A new Wheatsheaf was built at the back of the old Cheshire Cheese pub which for a time served as the entrance to the new Wheatsheaf. The former Cheshire Cheese housed a lounge bar with accommodation upstairs for the landlord and his family and was given a coat of plaster and white paint, which soon showed signs of damp and decay.

Subsidence was still an issue in Castle Street and an oft-told story tells how a hole opened up and swallowed a complete horse and cart in the road outside. When archaeologists looked at the area before redevelopment they found it totally covered by cinders and ash dumped into subsidence pits.

An extension to the rear was built to house the landlord and the front part was demolished for road widening. Until the 1980s it was still a fairly busy pub and the place to meet on Carnival Day, before or after a visit to the fair when goldfish hung in plastic bags all around it. It was allowed to stand empty and it was set on fire by arsonists.

An ancient wall is at the side of the Freemason's Arms and it is believed to be made from stones of the Roman wall of the fort, which was at first-floor level. The finding of the stones may well have suggested the name. A Roman road was traced in the garden at first-floor level and under the Oak Tree pub - which stood behind it.

This old photograph shows how the pub sits in an artificial cutting made in Victorian times to make the hill easier for horses with loaded carts. Within a matter of yards there were five other pubs and two off-licences! The Freemasons claim direct descent from the builders of Solomon's Temple but have no direct links with the pub.

On the boundary between the Northwich justices and Eddisbury ones, the Blue Barrel was ideally placed as a pub. Part of it, on the left, was demolished in 1929 when Darwin Street was built and an extension was added to the right. Why Darwin should have given his name to the street and his followers to its side streets is unknown.

In 1985 an excavation (just about) proved that the Blue Barrel stands on part of the Roman civilian settlement but produced pottery from the Civil War to the present. The first known landlord was recorded in 1643, the date that Sir Tomas Aston set up his camp in Castle after winning the Battle of Middlewich – he may have drunk here.

People always remark that the Thatched Tavern is not thatched. It takes its name from a former pub which stood where the white shed is now. That *was* thatched, and may have been part of a larger structure, which was reduced in size in 1870 when the railway line was built. The present pub was formerly three terraced cottages.

The Thatched Tavern Football Supporter's Club assembled in 1919. Many of the players in the team had not returned from the war but the enthusiasts continued to attend matches. These men are mainly too old or too young to have fought. Wearing a bowler (third row) is a bearded man resembling John Moore whose family ran the club for ninety-nine years.

Several cremated bodies were found here in 1838 and are still in their Roman urns at Chester and Warrington Museums. This photograph was taken when it was the Snooty Fox; it changed its name to the Rock Garden, but was closed when a male stripper asked an off duty police woman to remove his thong!

Opposite above: These two urns are now in the Grosvenor Museum at Chester but were discovered in the grounds of Winnington Lodge. They were made locally and the larger one has a dent where it rested against another pot in the kiln. The Roman ashes are still inside them.

Opposite below: The Snooty Fox was for a period the Grey Parrot, a residential club for ICI executives during the week and a place for birthday parties and receptions at the weekends. A feature was a large piano painted cream where famous guests signed their names. Among them were the Beatles who played in Northwich – pictured in 1974 at the carnival.

The stateliest drinking establishment in Northwich has to be Winnington Hall. Dating back centuries, this 1840s photograph shows the stone wing when it was a private girls' school. Among the visitors were John Ruskin the art critic and Hallé who founded the orchestra. For a time it was the exclusive ICI management club.

There was no pub in Winnington for over a century as Sir John Brunner, who co-founded Brunner and Mond, which later became ICI, did not approve. Yet a bar was provided for managers in the hall club, which is now a licensed restaurant. The Mond family lived in one wing and the Brunner's in the other – the families never mixed because of a feud over social status after Brunner married his housekeeper.

Brunner provided a social club for his workers, but without a bar. It was only when the committee pointed out that men were walking to bowling greens at pubs for a game and a drink that he allowed drinks to go with the sports. It must be the only drinking place locally with an old master – this is the boar hunt from the studio of Rubens. The rest of the Mond collection is in the National Gallery.

Hartford's two stations are three quarters of a mile apart as the railway companies whose lines cross there refused to have a joint station. The magistrates only allowed a pub next to the Greenbank in 1893 when three pubs in town were closed. The grand Victorian hotel featured a suite of private lounge/waiting rooms and refreshments.

Above: In 1837 the line from London to Glasgow opened with a main station at Hartford. Until the privatisation of British Rail, London–Glasgow trains still stopped at Hartford. The Station Hotel provided refreshments and hired transport to finish the journey. It is shown in this old photograph of the station above the covered walkway from the platform.

Left: One story tells of a rider carrying the Manchester mail, which had arrived here from London, who was shot by highwaymen. Another tells of the Prince of Wales (Edward VII) who frequently visited Hartford to stay with his friend the Earl of Enniskillen (pictured), master of foxhounds, to hunt foxes by day and 'vixens' at night.

Today the Station Hotel is renamed The Coachman and its stables are converted into a suite of residential rooms. Hartford's direct link with London ended when the railways were denationalised.

Whitegate and Marton once had three pubs. In teetotal and paternal Victorian times Lady Delamere objected to people coming out of service at the church to go to the pub on the village green. She closed it down and also one at the Beeches. As the Plough was opposite a teetotal Methodist chapel it was allowed to remain open, but not on a Sunday!

three

Along the Over Ridge

In 1971 a couple of workmen went into the Gate Inn one lunchtime and gave the landlady some old coins they had found for her daughter to play with. They went back to finish their work in Nixon Drive and the police were called in when they discovered a black cup full to overflowing with the coins.

Opposite above: Their find was declared treasure trove and is now one of the prize possessions of the Grosvenor Museum in Chester. They received £2,000 reward. The coins date from the time of Elizabeth I up to 1643, the year of the battle of Middlewich when the Roundheads camped in Northwich (see the Blue Barrel and Kings Arms).

Opposite below: Sir Thomas Aston 'sacked' Over in that year and it is said that he left rat poison wrapped up like sweets in the ruined cottages for the children to eat before losing the battle at Middlewich. It is not known if it was a villager who hid his savings or a Roundhead who hid his loot but whoever it was never went back to collect it.

Until 1874 the Mayor of Over was selected at the Cabbage Fair each spring and his first official task was to 'walk the fair' to inspect the stalls there. Afterwards he and the Court Leet dined at the George and Dragon. Every autumn he inspected the Onion Fair and also dined at the George and Dragon at Lord Delamere's expense.

THE CROSS. OVER CHESHIRE.

T.S.
B.&C.

"The Unique Series."

Above: The court could detain a drunk overnight in the prison cell under steps of the cross on the other side of the road. A story is told of there being a secret passage from the cell – despite the obvious reasons why this would be a silly idea! Nor is there any truth in the notion that it is Saxon despite the name Saxon Crossway.

Right: At the last Court Leet meeting in 1911 it was suggested that the mace be given to the new Winsford Council. Lord Delamere, who was there as Lord of the Manor, picked it up and refused, banging the table with the mace to make his point and breaking the staff. It was eventually sold to the council by his son in 1946 and is the one on the right.

The upstairs room at the George and Dragon was designed as a multi-use room but also to function as a town hall for Over. It was there every year that the election and appointment of the mayor took place over dinner. It was also the place for social events and for a variety of clubs to meet.

Opposite above: A brass band plays outside the Black Bear at 'Four Lane Ends' (now Over Square) at an unknown date before it closed in 1923. The fact that the Wheatsheaf was only on the other side of the road persuaded magistrates that there was one too many pub in the area. It is now a private house.

Opposite below: The ancient borough of Over in Delamere Street stands on glacial sand – which was ideal for wells – so it had its own brewery behind the Black Bear pub near Over Square and a mineral water factory opposite the George and Dragon. It might be that the dog's head over one of the doors at Saxon's is the trademark of a former brewery.

Above: Delamere Street before the First World War showing the Wheatsheaf on the left. A competition to find a new name in the 1980s quoted the mistaken belief that the cross in Delamere Street was Saxon – the real Saxon cross is in St Chad's Church. Its garish pink décor soon gave it the still often used name 'the Pink Palace'.

Left: After a fire at the cotton mill in Well Street where six people, including a mother and baby, died jumping from a top-floor window, the remains were taken to the stable at the Wheatsheaf, which became a makeshift mortuary. Only a few beads could be used by the coroner to identify one charred body.

Opposite below: In 1851 George Cross (land agent to the Vale Royal and Darnhall estates) took two half-barrels of beer in repayment for a debt at Darnhall. He used them to open a new pub on the estate, which remained in his family although they hired landlords to run it. His account books can be viewed on microfilm at Winsford Library.

The coroner's inquest was held at the Bull's Head at the end of Factory Street, which was renamed Geneva Road. The reason for the change is understandable – but why name it after Geneva? A flourishing new complex of streets was under construction for the workers, the houses were later used by men from the brickworks in High Street.

The Old Blue Bell is at the gate of St Chad's Church – which stands more than half a mile away from the village centre. Although nothing more than a cottage, it provided after-service refreshments to worshippers who had travelled long distances and also served as a working farmhouse. It is presumed that the refreshments were mainly taken to people in carriages outside.

Opposite above: The churchyard was extended in the early twentieth century, but in times gone by this area must have been a large open space opposite the tiny inn where carriages would wait during services and the refreshment orders could be delivered to them ready for the first food of the day at the end of service. On the extreme left is the hearse house.

Opposite below: The old inn is now used as a pre-school nursery although it is not the ancient pub. That was destroyed when fire broke out in the thatched roof and an exact replica was built in the 1970s. This picture was taken in the early 1920s when the old timber frame was hidden under a layer of bricks painted to look half timbered.

The people of OVER were good. The Devil was angry. He perceived their goodness was largely due to the excellent use they made of their Church. He determined to steal it that they might no longer worship there. One day he swooped down and flew off with the Church. But the people of OVER, accustomed to prayer, fell on their knees—the Devil's power was gone—he had only flown as far as the present site and was compelled to put the Church down there. Hence its curious position in a hollow in the fields away from the people. The moral is obvious.

St. Chad's Church, Over.

Left: Legend tells how St Chad's was stolen from the village by the Devil to prevent worship there, but the monks of Vale Royal caused him to drop it in the fields. The old parish extended as far south as Wettenhall, so a drink and something after morning service would be almost essential before travelling home.

Below: An aerial photograph shows the circular shape of the churchyard, which usually indicates a pre-Christian religious site which has been taken over by the Christians. The existence of a piece of Saxon cross here gave its name in error to the pub in Delamere Street. The church was a sanctuary for criminals on the edge of Delamere Forest

As the two sides of the river were administered as separate townships and were under different magistrates before 1874, there are sometimes two pubs of the same name in Winsford. This is the Blue Bell Inn which was at the end of Crook Lane in Wharton. It was a typical end-terrace cottage beer house serving a few local drinkers.

The Raven is still more often known as 'Th' Crow' and takes its name from the crest of the Corbet family who owned Darnhall in the early nineteenth century. It is a pun, since 'corbie' is a northern term for a raven. The microfilmed accounts of the estate (in Winsford Library) record beer purchased to refresh sheep-shearers in the 1830s.

The pretty timber-framed village of Church Minshull appears to have links with *The Wind in the Willows*, for the old Mill House is sometimes still called 't'owd hall' (the old hall) and has Frog Manor on the opposite side of the road. The pub name The Badger seems to echo this, but it is just coincidence.

The Badger was originally the Brooke's Arms, named after the owner of the village who lived at Norton Priory. It is in fact a rebus or punning coat of arms. Brooks (or 'Brocks' in dialect) was depicted by the crest of a badger or brock. In times when people could not read they would tell people to look for the badger – and the name stuck.

four

Winsford and Wharton

The Queen's Arms honoured Queen Victoria, and throughout the reigns of two Edwards and two Georges it remained the Queen's Arms. Not long after the present Queen came to the throne it was demolished to make way for Dean Drive and a new pub was built facing the fields where the new town centre was to be built.

The oldest building used as a pub in Winsford is Knight's Grange, although it only opened as a pub in 1971. The abbey farm was used as a farm until its lands were purchased to build the Grange Estate in the mid-1960s. Its brickwork is seventeenth century but inside is an older timber-framed wall. An alternative name in the Middle Ages was 'Bea Repair (nice place to go) – an ideal name for a pub.

Above: The parish boundary goes down the middle gable of the roof so you can stand at the bar in the parish of Over talking to someone in Whitegate. If you follow the lane to the railway bridge you are where the vicar of Over killed the Abbot of Vale Royal who was abducting a local girl. There is also a filled-in moat around the house.

Right: Many pubs have their slippery customers, but none more so than Tommy the toad. For many years he lived in the cellar at the White Swan on High Street and grew fat on the spiders and grubs he found there, as well as getting drunk on the spillages from the beer barrels. The dray-men always looked out in case they trod on him.

When the pub was due to be demolished to widen the road and the licence moved to a new pub in Wharton, Tommy was due to be taken to a new home there. He posed for photographs for the *Daily Mail* with a customer and the landlady, but as the pub was emptied before demolition there was no sign of him at all. Note the newspaper headline and Woodbines ashtray.

Opposite below: Dodd was subsequently expelled from the order because it was discovered that he had served the traditional harvest ale to his farm workers at Darnhall. During the harvest workers had weak beer, but at the end there was a party when strong harvest ale was served. In retaliation he opened his cottage as a beer house!

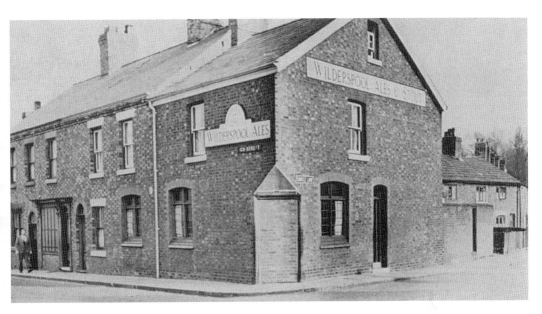

Rechabites' Row was made up of four cottages built in High Street by the teetotal Order of Rechabites, who took their name from an Old Testament tribe. Members often banded together to raise mortgages to build a group of houses and ran a 'tontine' (draw) to decide who moved in as each cottage was finished. Joseph Dodd had the final one.

Above: My reason for including this picture of the Weavers' Arms is that my grandfather's name is over the door as he was landlord from 1891-1897. When his first wife (pictured) died, as he could not read or write he had to leave the pub. Although my grandmother (his second wife) could read and write she was a teetotal Methodist so grandfather took to drink!

Left: This ale glass was engraved for use by my great grandmother; presumably at the Weavers' Arms. It is interesting to speculate on the name, for there does not seem to be a coat of arms for the river. However, there was a Weaver family of Weaver near Church Minshull as well as the weavers in the cotton mills.

Opposite below: The Navigation stood at the end of the Cheshire Lines branch line which carried wagons to the salt works. It was built when the line was also used for passengers in the nineteenth century. Today the line is a country walkway and the pub, which collapsed due to subsidence is replaced by a nightclub called 'The Liquid Lounge'.

There were a variety of friendly societies in the nineteenth century who only admitted fit men and then took a weekly subscription to pay for help in case of injury or ill health and to help with burial expenses. Most claimed ancient origins in the Bible, but the Foresters claimed the oldest of all and claimed Adam and Eve as the first members!

They say that there is only one house in Winsford and that's a pub. Until 1874 all addresses were either Wharton or Over except for the Red Lion which was simply addressed Winsford. It served a wharf on the Weaver from the eighteenth century and it is said that the river-cooled cellar gave the beer from the oak barrels a better flavour.

The Red Lion stands next to Winsford Bridge in an area which has almost totally changed in the last fifty years. The other building in this photograph is the Market Hall which later became Mr Smith's Club. Its once notorious supper licence let you purchase a portion of chips and then drink (and do other things!) until 2.00 a.m.

The Edwardian market place looks very respectable by day, but after dark its seven pubs and the fact that lone men from the boats on the river and coming home from the salt works went here for company gave a different reputation. No respectable woman would be seen there as it was the town's red light district. There are five pubs in this photograph.

The Swan, The Flatman's Tavern and The Ship were, as their names suggest, frequented by men from the 'flats' or salt barges on the river. It appears that all three were built at the same time to replace older pubs that had been damaged by subsidence. Later all the licences were taken away and the building was demolished.

The Royal Oak still stands in the Market Place, but you would find it difficult to recognise from this photograph of 1892. It is interesting to note that it has no chimney; instead four pipes come from the side walls indicating where enclosed fires burnt in 'pot-bellied boilers' as would have been used, as on a sailing barge for safety.

This photograph, taken about ten years later, shows that the whole exterior has been clad in hanging tiles to give an appearance of brickwork, and possibly as a safety measure. There is no use looking for the Royal Oak today for it functions as a nightclub. Opened in the 1970s as The Bees Knees, it is now known simply as D.B.'s.

The Ark is a handsome structure, again with stove pipes instead of a chimney; it is of interest as it still retains its traditional tongue and groove plank-lined rooms. In the past these were essential in Northwich and Winsford as they prevented bricks falling in on the customers in case of a sudden movement due to subsidence.

In the early 1960s the council published this imaginative illustration of how Winsford would look in the future. It shows they valued the Ark as a feature but the proposed continental drinking malls and tower blocks never materialised and the area has become something of a backwater except for late night revellers at D.B.s.

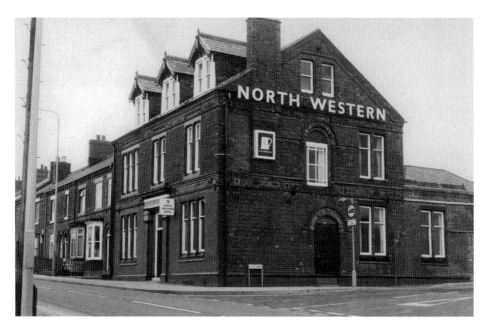

The North Western was the only pub on that side of Wharton, the others were along Station Road. As a child I imagined it was named after the local red buses, but it is actually named after the railway company whose goods line terminated over the road. Today its position at the top of the hill has caused a renaming to 'Top House'.

A side view shows the rear extensions, which served as the changing rooms for the teams from the nearby Barton Stadium which was not allowed to have a clubhouse or bar in the early years. On the other side of the road can just be glimpsed the retaining wall made from 1837 stone sleepers from the London North Western line.

The Princes Feathers is a reminder of the first prince to wear them, Edward I who founded
Vale Royal Abbey, but the link is unlikely to have suggested the name. In the 1980s the landlord
objected to the name as too royalist and renamed it Foggerty's after long-term landlord Harry
Foggerty (1939-69) – a prize fighter.

The Oddfellows, like the one in Davenham, takes its name from a friendly society first referred to
in the eighteenth century. They claim to have been founded by some 'old fellows' who formed a
saving club in a London inn in the fourteenth century. There is still an Oddfellows Society with a
national membership of savers.

Brighton Belle by Winsford Station was originally the Railway Inn and is a typical railway pub with a long stable block now used as a games room. It was renamed when a dining car from the old Brighton Belle was placed next to it for use as a dining room. It was removed in the 1990s, to rejoin the train, but the name remains.

When folk meet together, dissension to sow,
And breeding divisions encourage the foe,
When false motives, like colours, they hold to our view,
It's a sign they might find something better to do.

If ever the French should attempt to come here
To eat up our beef and drink our strong beer,
of both they'd fall short, but if fighting they wished,
At each sign of Middlewich they would be dished.

First the Lion called 'Golden' would make them quake,
And the Talbot no doubt would give them a shake,
At the sign of the 'Wolf' would they venture to rap,
They'd find, though too late, they's run into a trap.

By our bears, white and black they'd be put to the rout,
And a thrashing they'd get at the Wheatsheaf no doubt.
From the 'Lord Hood' a broadside they'd meet to their cost,
And at the 'Bull's Head' they'd be savagely tost.

At the White and Red Lions they'd find to their shame
Whether Black, White or Blue British lions are game.
At the 'Bridge Foot' they'd stop, and p'raps call for a 'whet'
And they'd get it – that is a good ducking they'd get!

If they call at 'The White Horse' they'll treat them so kind,
With a horse shoe, that more kicks than half-pence they'll find.
Should they venture to peep at the 'George and Dragon',
They'd see to their cost they'd got nothing to brag on.

Next at the 'Severn Stars' they'd soon show them the door,
At the 'Oak' a good drubbing they'd get – and no more.
Should these 'sans-coulottes' with our 'Crown' interpose,
They'd prick their French fingers well, under the 'Rose'.

At the 'Nag's Head' at bites and with cuffs they'd be treated,
At the 'Ring O' Bells' next with an empty house greeted;
The sign of the Eagle would raise fresh alarms,
And they'd run like soup maigre to escape the 'King's Arms',

May the sign of the 'King' ever meet with respect,
And our good constitution each Briton protect.
May he first caused all this trouble with France,
Be high hung on a sign, on nothing to dance.

Postscript, added 200 years later:

Only half of a dozen of these houses still remain
And just one of those has changed its old name.
Pub-crawling readers will find to their pleasure,
In mid-Cheshire now there are still pubs to treasure!

Above: The Big Lock is by the widest lock on this part of the Trent & Mersey Canal. Built into the bank, it has three stories at the back and had a separate entrance and bar on the canal side for the use of boat people during the day. There is also a long stable block or their horses in winter with a hay store above.

Right: Facing Webb's Lane the pub presents a more traditional front. When the downstairs bar closed in the evening the upstairs one opened as a traditional pub with bar and lounge facilities, just like any other. Today it has been extended into the stables and there is now no distinction between upstairs and downstairs drinking areas.

Opposite: These patriotic verses were composed in Middlewich at the time of the plans for invasion by Napoleon of France. Many of the references are to Napoleon and the Revolution. It is reproduced from C.F. Lawrence, *A History of Middlewich*, 1895.

The Vaults is an old pub that was almost totally rebuilt when the bypass was built in the 1960s. Beyond in Wheelock Street is the White Bear and to the left of where the photographer is standing used to be the Black Bear. The photograph was taken from the old Bull Ring where bulls and bears were baited until the nineteenth century.

Unlike the bulls, who were killed for the butchers shops which surrounded the ring, the bear would sometimes join his owner for a drink in one of the bear pubs afterwards. One tale tells how a bearward had his goods taken by a constable, so he took the bear as 'a lady visitor' to see the constable. The constable hid up the chimney and the bearward left town with his bear.

The bear is still portrayed in a carving over the arch to the impressive late Victorian stable yard with accommodation for carriages and stables for horses. The pebble-dash and timbering in an arts and crafts style betray the presence of a much older establishment behind the front.

The Navigation stood by the bridge and recalls the canal builders. It was another two-level structure – the difference is clear from the policeman and the landlady. As well as serving as a split-level pub it was also a shop and sold hay and straw for the barge-horses on the canal tow path.

The King's Arms never changed its name, even for Queen Victoria, though it stands on the corner of Queen Street. This was formerly Dog Lane and during the Battle of Middlewich in 1643 a canon faced along it – the Roundheads, however, came along Booth's Lane. It still has timber-frame walls behind the Edwardian façade.

Above: In the middle of the nineteenth century it was another pub with a dual use. Not only did it serve beer, wines and spirits, but it was also the local Inland Revenue office. People had to come here to pay their taxes and to pay the excise duty on legal documents and publicans on the spirits sold in their pubs.

Right: The Boar's Head takes its name from the Vernon family who owned Kinderton Hall and much of Middlewich in the eighteenth century. The family never lived in the town, and are best known for the elopement of Dorothy Vernon at Haddon Hall. This fine arts and crafts façade was created when it was the main hotel at the entrance to the town.

It is ironic that the Talbot was on the other side of the road from the Boar's Head as this is the name and emblem of the Earls of Shrewsbury. It was the heir to this title who was being married to Dorothy Vernon's sister at the time of the famous elopement. It went to make way for road widening around 1970.

The King's Lock is another split-level pub: the rear faces a short arm of the canal once used as a dock, the front faces a raised part of the canal. Its isolated position in fact makes the bridge by the lock the only way of getting to and from it. It is by the junction of the Trent & Mersey and the Shropshire Union and was built by James Brindley.

six

A Village
Pub Crawl

The Crown at Lower Peover is an attractive old farm pub by the main road from Middlewich to Knutsford, with a sad tale. It is told on an old gravestone in Prestbury Churchyard where they buried little Frances Rathbone in 1721. She had been sent on an errand to a local shop, apparently lost her way and was found dead under a hedge in Peover.

The body was carried to the Crown. There had been a thunderstorm the night before and people recalled seeing the girl and even turning her away. No wonder the gravestone reads 'Well might the thunder rend the air to see such monsters living there. Thrice helpless child thus doomed to roam and leave thy every friend at home'.

Right: The Bells of Peover were not those that hang in the church tower, but were a family who kept it as the Warren de Tabley Arms in the nineteenth century and ran a brewery there. The de Tabley coat of arms is still on the wall, between the flags of England and the USA. They record the presence here of many Americans during the Second World War.

Below: This nineteenth-century painting, which hangs above a fireplace in the pub, shows its position at the side of the churchyard very clearly, and to the left can be seen the bell of the little eighteenth-century school. It is said that it stands on the site of the medieval priest's house and this gave rise to a strange tradition.

Left: Until the north chapel was converted to a vestry there was nowhere for the choir to put on their robes. Until Victorian times that did not matter as they did not wear special clothes, but it later became a problem. The answer was on hand though: after service the vicar and choir would walk out of the tower door and the short distance to the pub to disrobe.

Below: This early nineteenth-century print shows the black and white appearance of the church is not as old as the thirteenth-century timber interior. Besides showing the Bells and school it illustrates another odd feature of the church. The slab wall around the church is unique in Cheshire, but resembles sacred enclosures in places like Ireland.

During the Second World War General Patton had his headquarters at Peover Hall and used the Bells regularly. He met General Eisenhower in the lounge shown in this drawing of 1948. Many American troops were stationed in the North West during the build up to D-Day so that the Germans could only guess at where the landings might be.

The Duke of Portland at Lach Dennis is named after an eighteenth-century soldier duke who set his long-serving sergeants up as landlords of their own pubs, thus ensuring that they could earn a living after retiring from the army. There are a number of Dukes of Portland throughout England where his NCOs returned to their homes.

The duke was close to the unenclosed land known as Rudheath (not to be confused with the Northwich estate). Romper Lowe, the head of a gang of poachers, would sit in the pub with his traps and nets as if to go out poaching, while the sheriff's men watched. Meanwhile his gang were busy poaching in the woods unobserved.

Now in the Rudheath housing estate, the Broken Cross was built where the Middlewich road crossed the Trent & Mersey, a busy wharf for goods to and from Northwich in the eighteenth century. Its name may be because the canal broke through a crossroads rather than because of a broken structure. You can still see the four disjointed roads that meet by the bridge.

An early twentieth-century photograph of the Bull's Head in Davenham shows the power of advertising, which was a Victorian obsession. Some of the lettering may still be seen, but the main difference between this turn-of-the-century photograph and a modern one is the house, which appears to join the pub to its separate stable block, has gone.

A 1970s postcard shows the alterations including a new door into the tap room. An entrance drive to a rear car park has also been made through the adjoining second stable block, which is used as a dining area today.

Of interest, although often obscured by parked cars, is the cobblestone forecourt. Cobbles were created by the ice sheets of the Ice Age over 10,000 years ago and are often found if digging locally. In Victorian times children were paid to follow the plough and collect them. Road makers paid ¼d for a bucketful.

The Lion (pictured) and the Traveller's Rest in Moulton were both opened in the early 1890s. Before then Moulton had been a strictly teetotal factory village serving salt works in the Weaver Valley. The Verdin family, who were salt makers, encouraged an influx of new villagers at the time and ensured customers for the pubs. Many came from the south of England.

Perhaps this influx of new residents who had been displaced from farming areas by the introduction of machines suggested the name Traveller's. The Moulton Crows were a team of male dancers who performed at local fetes dressed as crows until the 1950s – the restaurant was named after them.

There were two pubs which had stood at 'Four Lane Ends' in Lostock from the eighteenth century until the road was widened in 1937. The Black Greyhound and the Slow and Easy are both shown on the right of this photograph. Slow and Easy are said to have been the names of two carthorses, but might indicate the pace of drinking.

The Black Greyhound takes its name from a local coat of arms. It was used by the Holfords until the last heiress, Lady Mary, married into the Cholmondeley family and moved to Vale Royal. It was subsequently used by the Lostock family. The coach to Northwich is pictured in Edwardian times.

Lady Mary Cholmondeley (*née* Holford) was known as The Bolde Lady of Cheshire. After she entertained James I at Vale Royal he offered to take her sons to court, but she refused the offer – possibly concerned about tales of immorality there. She lived at Holford Hall, but built Knight's Grange in Winsford for her younger son. The black greyhound was his family coat of arms.

A new Black Greyhound in 'roadhouse' style was built at the next crossroads in Wincham in 1938. It had a large wooden function room in the car park – known as the 'Ponderosa' after the ranch in the television western series.

One of the oldest hostelries to survive is the Smoker at Plumley. Now fronted by a busy dual carriageway, it retains its thatched roof with a wing roofed in Kerridge slabs from near Macclesfield. It is named after Lord de Tabley's horse. The idea of a smoking horse might make you think of one with a cough – but it was smoky grey!

Great Budworth was extensively remodelled in the arts and crafts style by Piers Egerton Warburton of Arley and his friend the architect John Douglas of Sandiway. Almost all the cottages were rebuilt or reconstructed by the pair and the George and Dragon was remodelled in the latest style as a better-class hotel.

Left: To control drinking in the village the other pubs were closed down. To underline the message of moderation in drinking, above the door was placed the inscription: 'As St George in arm'd array did the fiery dragon slay, so might thou with might no less, slay that dragon drunkenness.'

Below: The Great Budworth annual wakes festival was stopped when too many drinking townspeople attended and as a final hint of sobriety the pub was run for four generations by a family called Drinkwater. The sign was made by a blacksmith in Bavaria and is copied from a golden sovereign of Queen Victoria.

Antrobus in the parish is known for the traditional Souling Play which is performed in pubs around the village at the start of December. The traditional characters include a mock battle between King (Saint) George and a black-faced 'Moor' and the appearance of the wild horse in a mock auction at the end of the play which was performed at the George.

This cottage was formerly the Ring O' Bells pub, which along with the Saracen's Head closed down in 1856 to concentrate drinking under control at the George next door. It is of especial interest as the old half-timbered front (with a date of 1711 scratched on it) is backed by a late nineteenth-century arts and crafts-style rear.

A watercolour in The Salt Museum shows the White Hart on High Street with a view of Budworth Church in 1853. The pub closed in 1861 as drinking was centred on the George. It is believed that the artist might have been art tutor to the young Piers Warburton and the painting forms part of a collection of his works about the village.

One of the best-known stops on the coaching route from London to Warrington was the Cock at Budworth. It is not actually in the village and so escaped the closures as its main customers were travellers. It was an important staging inn until the advent of the railways but became popular again with the growth of cycling and motoring.

Above: Drunken Barnaby called at the Cock on his journey to the North of England in the eighteenth century. He records his visit in verse: 'Thence to the Cock at Budworth where I drank strong ale as brown as a berry, till at last with deep healths felled, to my bed I was compelled, I for state was bravely sorted, by two porters well supported.'

Right: The Stanley Arms at Anderton takes its name from the nineteenth-century owners of Winnington Hall, which it looks down on. Its common name is The Tip, not for the want of housekeeping, but because for 100 years until the Anderton Lift was built a series of long slides were used to tip goods from the canal boat into river boats.

This mid-nineteenth century view of Anderton shows the tips which took pottery and salt from the canal at the top of the bank and slid them into the holds of vessels on the Weaver. It also shows an inclined plane (left), an uphill railway line used to take goods up the bank. The house in the centre might be the Stanley Arms.

Left: The pub sign shows the arms of Stanley with the 'brid and babby' crest (see the Eagle and Child, Northwich). Lord Stanley was a campaigner for social improvement after the Irish potato famine and arranged for poor families to be sent to live in America. See *The Ladies of Alderley* by Nancy Mitford.

Opposite below: The Navigation was on the canal bank and had a pub for the bargemen and a shop for their purchases next door. At 'the Tunnel Mouth' a small community of traders built up relying on the bargees, including clogmakers and ropemakers. The pub closed in 1959 just three years before the 'big freeze' ended commercial us of canals.

Barnton Tunnel was one of three that were needed to take the canal to Runcorn. To prevent barges from the Weaver ever using it the Duke of Bridgewater ensured it was only wide enough to take one barge at a time. Queues of barges would build up and wait at the canalside pubs while a one-way system operated.

Left: The Reaper's Arms was a beer house which stood above the tunnel at Barnton and allowed the man leading the horse to make a quick stop for refreshments while his colleagues undertook the more laborious task of 'legging' the barge – often in a queue – through the tunnel below.

Below: The Ring O' Bells stood by the churchyard gate at Weaverham until 1924. The new building was built to serve the expanding housing estates in the village at that date. In Victorian times the Virgin's Club met there until meetings were stopped because of too much drinking. The name related to the Virgin Mary – not to the all-female members.

From the 1920s Weaverham expanded from a small village into one of the biggest in the country as ICI took advantage of government schemes to provide workers housing for people who had jobs to go to. Weaverham expanded as the Winnington Works did and the Ring O' Bells became the local for the new estates.

The Wheatsheaf has an attractive late eighteenth-century exterior. It still has an unusual reminder of the past in that the front room is named 'Knowledge Room' over the entrance. It was also sometimes called 'Parliament' and for years it was the place for village discussion and debate over current affairs, nationally and locally.

The origins of the Knowledge Room lie in the years after the French Revolution when the Government banned public libraries and taxed printed material so high that the poor could not afford it in case it promoted revolution. The room contained a small reference library and newspapers were purchased from a weekly collection.

Besides being on the main A49 trunk road through the parish of Weaverham, the Gate can also be seen as the gateway to Weaverham, a role that this picture of an Edwardian rose fete illustrates. The man with the gun on the right is pushing a decorated cycle; these featured in most local processions until the 1930s.

Above: A photograph from the end of the nineteenth century shows the Gate almost as it is today, except that modern safety on a bend with a narrow pavement has meant that the Gate sign has been removed. The 'gallows' beam from which it once hung remains, complete with a bunch of grapes to indicate that wine was on sale.

Opposite below: The name Weaverham Gate is far older than the pub, even though John Wesley recorded staying there in the eighteenth century. It takes its name from the main highway or 'yate' in old English. The exterior is very much as Wesley would have known it and even has a mounting block cut from a sandstone weight from a cheese press.

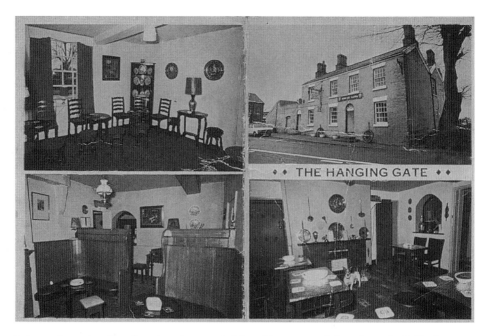

It is rare for an interior of a pub to be recorded, but this menu card from the early 1970s shows the former interior of the Gate. Of interest are the built-in oak settles which created atmospheric drinking areas in the lounge and the sparse arrangement of chairs and tables in the tap room.

The White Barn at Cuddington is believed to take its name from an ancient barn used by salters travelling from Northwich with their packhorses loaded with white salt. The building was rebuilt as a coaching stop and then became the station pub when the railway came to the village in 1870.

A seventeenth-century engraving of a chain of packhorses carrying goods, including salt. It was believed that the White Barn was built to house the salt horses and it links to other names including white and salt which show the way of these packhorse trains before the days of railways and canals.

"THE BLUE CAP"

The traditional first meeting place for the Cheshire Hunt each season was at the Blue Cap opposite to their kennels. Children were given the day off school to watch and run errands. Carriages and later motor cars would follow the hounds at the start of the hunt.

It is said that all the Cheshire hounds are descended from Blue Cap, the hound belonging to the Hon. J. Barry of Marbury Hall. Blue Cap won a race at Newmarket in 1762 against Wanton, the pride of the Quorn Hunt from Leicestershire, taking the £1,000 stake. It is said that he was given a weighted collar to wear when hunting to keep him at the speed of the rest of the pack.

Blue Cap was buried in the pub garden. His monument was in the garden until it was taken to the kennels of the Cheshire Hunt in the 1950s to stop curious visitors who did not buy a drink. This party appears to date from the 1920s.

Right: Apart from Kennel Lane where Blue Cap's monument with a rhyming epitaph by Egerton Warburton of Arley is now, Cock Pit Lane is also opposite the pub. This cock fighter's clay pipe is one of several found there in the 1960s and now in the Salt Museum collection. The pub was called Sandiway Head until the nineteenth century.

Below: It is worth a slight detour to include the Abbey Arms at Oakmere as it once contained the court house where pub licences for the area were granted. The sandstone building is of eighteenth-century date and is one of the few mid-Cheshire Buildings made of stone which occurs along the central Cheshire ridge of hills.

Above: Queen Aetheflaeda, the daughter of King Alfred, founded a defensive town on Eddisbury Hill and in the Middle Ages justice was administered from the Chamber in the Forest on the Hill. The pub became the centre of justice for the Eddisbury region until Delamere Police Station with its court house and cells was built.

Left: The arms of Vale Royal Abbey include the three lions of England with the abbot's crosier to show the royal links. The Vale Royal accounts show that Lord Delamere paid for a 'soup kitchen' here in the famine of the 1840s. The choice of the pub as a centre of justice is probably because the forest was a sanctuary for criminals until 1812.

Right: Thomas Walker, a Manchester tailor, saved all the off-cuts from the clothes he made and charged the customer by the length of cloth including the off-cuts. This was his profit – known as 'cabbage' in the trade – and was used to make up garments using the pieces. With his extra profits he was able to open a pub on the main A49 route.

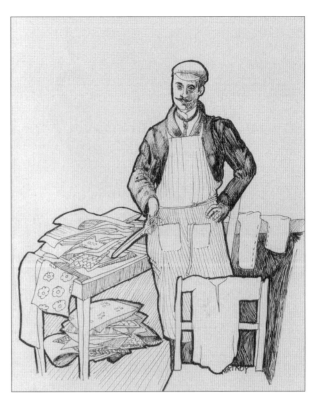

Below: Cabbage Hall has been much enlarged since his day, and another tale lurks in Longstone Lane near by. By its side is the 'headless cross' re-sited from near the pub. According to one of Nixon's Cheshire prophesies a raven will one day sit on its top and be able to drink the blood of the victims of a great and decisive battle!

Left: The Fishpool at Delamere is not named after Oakmere, but after a series of former pools used by the monks of Vale Royal. Mature fish were allowed to spawn and after a year were moved into the next pool, the following year they went to the spawning pool. As they were hand fed it was easy to catch them by hand!

Below: The Red Lion Inn faces the church at Little Budworth and has done for almost 200 years. There is nothing surprising about a pub by a church, until you realise that the churchyard – and the graves in it – sits on top of a stone retaining wall, putting the living and the dead level. Its age is uncertain, but it might indicate that the church stands on a prehistoric burial mound.

Above: Prophet Nixon, who always foretold gloom and doom, said 'beware the lord of Oulton, lest you be hung at your gate'. In the way that aristocrats had of getting out of unpleasant prophesies, the family coat of arms is above the gate and hangs outside the Egerton Arms. The hall and the lord have gone – but the sign is still there.

Right: Sammy Grice was, in the non-PC language of the nineteenth century 'a half idiot dwarf' who lived in Chester. He was ridiculed by some and pitied by others, but made a living making wooden meat skewers and pegs to ventilate the cork bungs of beer barrels. He died in 1811, and is said to have given his name to the 'Little Man o' Wettenhall'.

In 1843 it appears the pub may have been known as the Pig and Whistle, a common name taking its name from a type of beer mug called a 'piggin' which had a whistle in the handle. There are older records still of a 'Little Robin Hood' in Wettenhall, so the origins of the name are far from certain.

The figure of the Little Man is made in fine terracotta work and set into the front of the pub and was probably made in the Ruabon brickworks. The figure actually resembles John Bull and it could be possible that it was merely a decorative feature which was adopted as the pub name in an age when people could not read.

Above: In 1848 the Boot and Slipper is recorded as the Royal Oak. It might be that the oak tree in the car park is one of numerous trees grown from acorns of the Royal Oak at Boscobel in Worcester where Charles I hid after the Battle of Worcester. There appears to be evidence that the name Boot and Slipper is an old one revived.

Right: The slipper is not a carpet slipper, but was used in the past to indicate a slip-on lady's shoe, as in Cinderella's glass one. We still put model slippers on a wedding cake and tie boots behind the bridal car. It would seem likely that the name was in honour of a wedding, but whose and when is not recorded.

Other local titles published by Tempus

Crewe Pubs

HOWARD CURRAN

Illustrated with over 100 old photographs and postcards, this book traces some of the changes and developments of public houses, and highlights a variety of architectural styles and past ways of life in the town. From The Chetewood Arms and The Royal Oak in the 1900s to the Bridge Inn and Spread Eagle in the 1960s, each picture recalls the varied social history of the area and offers an insight into the popularity and changing role of such well-known establishments.

0 7524 3254 0

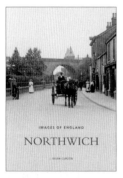

Congleton History & Guide

JOAN ALCOCK

Many Congleton residents will know the story of how the townspeople sold their Bible in the seventeenth century in order to buy a new bear, but details of other episodes from the town's history may be less well known. This engaging study, illustrated with over 100 photographs and a variety of other archive material, presents for the first time a chronological history of this Cheshire market town from Neolithic times to the twenty-first century.

0 7524 2946 9

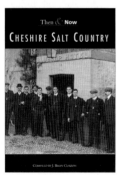

Northwich

J. BRIAN CURZON

This splendid collection of over 150 archive images documents some of the major events and changes that have occurred in Northwich over the years, mainly from the end of the nineteenth century through to local government reforms in 1973. J. Brian Curzon is a prolific writer on Cheshire history. Each image in this volume is accompanied by detailed and informative text detailing the rich history of Northwich.

0 7524 3149 8

Cheshire Salt Country Then & Now

J. BRIAN CURZON

The three salt towns of Winsford, Northwich and Middlewich have witnessed great changes over the past century. By contrasting old photographs with up-to-date images these eighty pairs of images offer the reader a glimpse of the social and economic changes which have occurred in this area of Cheshire.

0 7524 2675 3

If you are interested in purchasing other books published by Tempus, or in case you have difficulty finding any Tempus books in your local bookshop, you can also place orders directly through our website

www.tempus-publishing.com